In these ter
childhood, Winifred Foley :
small mining community in the 1920 s. Humour
pathos and tragedy are deftly interwoven in this
sequel to 'A Child in the Forest'.

Also by Winifred Foley:

A Child in the Forest
Back to the Forest
In and Out of the Forest

No Pipe Dreams for Father

for Father

Scenes from a Forest of Dean Village Childhood

No Pipe Dreams for Father

Scenes from a Forest of Dean Village Childhood

by

Winifred Foley

With an introduction by Humphrey Phelps
Illustrated by A. G. Edwards

Douglas McLean Publishing
Cole ford, Gloucestershire
www.forestbookshop.com

First Published in Great Britain by Douglas McLean in 1977
This Edition published by Douglas McLean 2002
Reprinted November 2006

First Futura Publications Edition 1978
Including additional material *(Dashed Hopes, Kezzie* and *Our Scott)* by
Winifred Foley
Reprinted 1979, 1982

Our Scott first appeared in the January 1978 edition of Gloucestershire
Life

ISBN 0 946252 40 8

Printed and Bound i⸺
Ashford Press, South⸺

Published by
Douglas McLean
8 St John Streeet
Coleford
Gloucestershire
England
GL16 8AR

TO MY FRIENDS

Foreword

A Child in the Forest brought fame and success to Winifred Foley, but she is still shy and modest; in essence she is still a child of the Forest. In these tales about the Forest she writes with a touching simplicity and a childlike honesty that is altogether charming.

All of these tales are apparently slight but they have the power to move the reader to an occasional chuckle and, more often, to the verge of tears.

Older readers will remember that dread phrase which occurs in one story – "Im 'ave got it.' It is a mark of real progress that younger readers are not familiar with it. If this book does nothing else it should at least make us pause and count our blessings. But it also exemplifies – and Winifred herself is a good example – that even hardships and grinding poverty could not quench the human spirit; kindliness, comradeship, hope and joy still came bubbling out.

I'm sure that Winifred Foley's many admirers will welcome this little book but, like me, wish there'd been more about old Auntie and Granny. And Jarge, who was unlearned in the misuse of words. But I've kept you from Winifred Foley for long enough . . . . . .

Humphrey Phelps

Author's Note

How nice it was to be asked by a Forest publisher to write a second book of personal and garnered memories of life in the Forest of Dean some fifty odd years ago, and then to get the special bonus of two talented Forest artists, A.G. Edwards to illustrate the stories, and Douglas Eaton for the delightfully evocative cover.

Be it slum or palace, nostalgia is almost inevitable for the place where one grows up. My early years in that corner of England, so lush with flora and fauna, called the Forest of Dean remains for me and many others an evergreen memory. Thanks to all concerned with this book for enabling some of these memories to get into print.

Winifred Foley

Preface to This Edition

It is a quarter of a century since Douglas McLean first published this book. Now in my 89th year I feel closer to 'that bourne from which no traveller returns.' As is usual with the elderly, I cannot remember from one minute to the next where I have put my specs, my puffer, my stick and suchlike – yet the memories of my youth get more vivid as time marches on. These tales are from my childhood spent in poverty in a small mining village in the Forest of Dean and oh, how I remember how rich it was in the beauty of the landscape and the wonderful character of its people. Some were good, some not so good and some were truly marvellous folk that I feel so privileged to have known and loved.

And how times have changed! We are incomparably richer in material luxuries and incomparably poorer in human relationships.

We no longer have time to sit around each others' hearths sharing the joys and the humour and helping to heal each others' heartbreaks. Among our products of progress is that robot intruder the television, which rules our leisure and feeds on our time. Also of course, we now have central heating at the touch of a button. Washing machines, cars, telephones and air travel are part of everyday life. However, we also have incredibly efficient means of making war. The widespread presence of nuclear warheads has given humanity the jitters. If only we would heed the old saying 'Be good and let those who will be clever'.

Winifred Foley
Cheltenham 2002

A Washing Day

It was the worst day of the week. It was washing day and the signs were ominous. True the weather was dry, but it was worried by a spiteful icy wind. Mother was already in a lather carrying buckets of water through our little living-room to fill the copper in the dark back-kitchen. Old Auntie was irritated at the small amount of rainwater in the brick-lined covered well, outside the front door, that housed the precious water from our cottage's guttering.

Old Auntie was a washer of the old school, a believer in starching, blueing, and plenty of rinsing. Mother, who would work like a Trojan at the dollying and scrubbing, had no time for such laundering refinements. She was glad to get it washed at any price. Intolerant of each other's methods, they were as likely to come to the boil as the whites in the copper. They would have a row before the day was out, and treat each other to a list of their respective shortcomings in all directions.

The fire in the big black-leaded grate had the miseries, too, suffocated as it was by a huge black iron saucepan full of swede and potato peel and coarse cabbage, boiling to add to the bran in the bucket for the pigs' dinner. My sister had been packed off to school in a bad humour because the pair of drawers old Auntie had made her from some striped flannelette 'is showin' all down below me frock'.

My toddler brother was crying to be picked up. Mother, heavy with child, could hardly find room to squeeze with her loaded buckets between the table and chairs. The last thing she wanted was an un-cooperative three-year-old who had soaked up the atmosphere of tension and irritability. 'Now get from under my feet,' Mam warned me as I stood by the copper while she tried to poke the fire beneath it to a blaze. Determined to help, I threw a pair of my sister's black woollen school stockings into the copper among the whites when Mam had to rush to the kitchen. The saucepan of pigs' food had tipped into the fire, and poor Auntie had not the strength in her rheumaticky old hands to straighten it.

'I'll get the little varmint outside,' said old Auntie, and wrapping me up in a parcel of old scarves, she shoved me outside with a couple of currants in a piece of paper. With a mutinous scowl I sat on top of the stone steps leading up to the garden. My nose was level with a group of early narcissi and their perfume drew it to their white-petalled beauty and the thin scarlet edgings of their trumpet centres. At three years old I felt 'drunk' for the first time, intoxicated by a little piece of nature's living artistry.

18

The coldness of the stone step on my bum soon sobered me up and I crept indoors again.

Old Auntie had poured the saucepan of pigs' scraps into the bucket with the bran, where it waited to cool enough for Mam to take it to the pigs, and now she had got my little brother on her lap, soothing him to sleep. To sit over that steaming bucket would be just the job to warm my bum, I thought, and I knew that her arthritics and having my brother on her lap would prevent her stopping me for a bit. I ignored her warnings and edged myself over the bucket. Just a little too far: my behind, and a whole lot more of me, got a warm-up as down I went into the mushy smelly contents. Wedged a prisoner, there I sat till Mam rushed out from the back-kitchen and truly hotted up my nether end with her soapy hands.

'That's all I be short of, a yup more washin', Mam wailed as she peeled my clothes off. 'I know what we'll do,' said old Auntie, 'we'll shut the little toe-rag up in the front room.'

The front room was a narrow slip of a room which contained old Auntie's single bed, her finest piece of furniture, a mahogany chest of drawers with glass knobs, a small wooden table under the window, and a couple of chairs. There was also a hanging basket over the window, from which grew a trailing plant much cosseted and watered, and old Auntie's family Bible.

Re-dressed in what Mam could find me, I was pushed inside and the door locked. Kicking and banging brought no response. Presently, from the back-kitchen, I could hear the two women's voices raised in argument. All the washing in the copper had boiled to a dingy greyish-blue. Mam had fished out a pair of ruined, once-black, woollen stockings, and now each was blaming the other for putting them in with the whites. Suddenly Mam exclaimed, 'I'll warrant it was that little tartar in the front room what done it. I'll give 'er the good 'idin' of 'er life, that I will.' Mam's mood made Auntie act in defence council on my behalf till she had cooled off. 'Leave 'er be till we 'ave finished the weshin'! Anyroads, non ont'll need the blue bag for a bit.'

Unrepentant, my martyrdom increased. 'I'll rip your bloody plant down if you don't let me out,' I yelled as they came within earshot. 'Doosn't take any notice on 'er,' advised old Auntie; "er can't reach up to touch'n.'

I couldn't, but there was the chair to climb on, and the little table. Not quite tall enough, so I took the chair, and from it reached the Bible off the chest of drawers. It was a huge illustrated volume with metal clasps to shut it. I struggled and heaved it on to the table, then tiptoed to reach some of the trailing foliage and ripped at it with all my energy.

I knew I was in for a good hiding, I intended to have my hide's worth! When they opened the door, I intended to get under the far corner of the bed. They would have to drag me out! My apprehension soon changed to hope when I heard the sound of Father's heavy pit boots across the yard. I put back my head, opened my mouth, and began to howl piteously.

'What's all this then? What's goin' on?' asked Father as he unlocked the door and picked me up in his dirty pit clothes. 'That's right,' said Mam sharply. 'Make me a bit more weshin', as though the little 'ussy ain't made me enough already.'

I sniffed and sobbed as tragically as an Ophelia, whilst Mam listed my misdemeanours of the day, interrupted by a little scream of horror from old Auntie. 'Me plant, me plant! Er 'ave ruined me plant!' I clung tightly to the refuge of Dad's neck whilst he inspected my horticultural rape.

'Now, doosn't thee fret, Aunt. I 'a' bin meanin' to prune thic plant f'r a long time. Thee see, 'im'll shoot out better'n ever now.' Father put me down and followed Mam into the back-kitchen. There was some whispering, and sound of kissing going on, and Mam came out looking all soppy with her mouth twitching at the corners as it did when she had a nice secret all to herself.

Dad sat down at the table, took my little brother in the crook of one arm and me on the other knee, and began to eat his boiled-egg tea. Times were hard, but never in my life did I ever hear Dad complain about whatever Mam could muster up for him to eat. Enthroned on his lap I ate the bits of crust he broke from his own bread and butter and dripping in the yoke of his egg, a bit for my brother and a bit for me.

Naughty, undeserving, I drank the tea he poured into his saucer, but I remember . . . I remember . . .

Early One Morning

The feather bed, made from plucked chicken feathers by ancestral grannies, was warm and soft. My sister, little brother and I slept in its dents as cosy as beans in their fur-lined pods. Winter and summer, Mam had quite a job prising us out of it.

From our little back bedroom it was hard to see what season it was. The bottom of the tiny window rested on the garden level of the cottage above ours, and weeds often obstructed our minute view.

On school mornings our Mam kept calling up the stairs threatening us with the stick on our behinds to start out with, and very likely the same from the headmaster at the other end, if we were late for school. We became quite expert at measuring the irritation in Mam's voice, and we mostly timed our jumps out of bed just as she started up the stairs. We thought of a good ploy to fool her by banging our boots on the wooden floor without actually leaving the bed, but it did not always work!

On summer mornings, once up, it seemed just as good as being in bed. My sister and I washed first, in the little dark back-kitchen. Our little brother could take his time; he was still too young for a stint of water carrying before breakfast.

My sister had a proper yoke with a bucket at each end, and I had two wire-handled tins. Mam would be getting our breakfast, toast done in front of the fire bars and kept warm on the hob, while we went down the garden path, then through the gently sloping woodland, and down to the well at the side of the main road. Converging from other paths, we could hear the voices of other children on the same errand.

The pure, exhilarating morning air, the sunshine benediction, and the thought of the warm toast to come, plus our sleep-renewed energies, often drove us mad with joy. In those days, wild sweet days, we had the privilege to behave like lunatics. We could yell our heads off, take running jumps into the lush green fern between the trees, make drums out of our buckets with banging sticks, and pause to look at all the wonders along the way.

'Look at this bloody yup under 'ere!' The flat upturned stone revealed a mass of sluggish wood-lice. Poor stupid things, hiding from the summer's day! Whatever did they do all day! Unlucky creatures. Lower the stone again, very carefully, not to squash them. Oh, how lucky I was, born me instead of wood lice!

'Eh, thee come 'n zee wot I 'ave found. The cu'st 'a some, there's plenty a growin' just 'ere.' We picked and relished the pale green juicy sharp-tanged leaves

of something we knew as wood-sorrel. It often
sharpened our imaginations as well as our taste
buds.

'Coo, I just zeen a girt great fox over there, wi'
blood round 'is chops. 'Im 'ave 'id behind thic tree
over there.'

We knew it was not true, but in an ecstasy of
terror we would run screaming down to the well.
Fear-tightened throats were soon eased with cupped
handfuls of sparkling spring water. In the mossy
stream from the well overflow we observed the

progress of the black spot in the frog spawn, via the tadpole to the endearing ugly croaking frog; a fairy prince, of course, under a witch's spell.

Water slopped out of our containers as we raced to pluck the rare white foxglove amid the myriads of pinky-purple ones growing among the ferns. These special ones were for Teacher.

By the time I heaved my tins on to the back-kitchen table, the water content was well down.

Toast in hand, and off up the hill to school. Spring brought the leggy lambs running up to their mothers for short and urgent sucking sessions. We saw the afterbirths, we knew that hens laid eggs and that baby pigs came out of the mother sow, but we never doubted that we were young, God-like creatures, mysteriously deposited under the gooseberry bush to be brought to our mothers in the midwife's bag. How I scolded Mam on one occasion for just lying in bed all day with our new-born baby when she should have been getting our tea. That she must be there to keep him warm seemed a poor excuse.

Autumn brought the fluttering leaves, piled by the winds into the banks of confetti to jump and roll in and scatter back to the winds.

Winter seeped through our boots, aggravating our itching chilblains, but they were soon forgotten in the snowball pelting with our 'enemies'. Icicles made lovely lolly-ices to suck, but summer mornings were the best of all, mornings to recapture when I listen now to the evocative genius of Beethoven's 'Pastoral' Symphony, taking me back to the well-springs of my childhood, to fetching water from the well.

No Pipe Dreams for Father

I stood with uncharacteristic patience whilst Mam tied up my pinny into a sort of pocket, put old Auntie's pension book in it, then made it extra safe with two large safety pins. I was going on a very important errand and well aware of it!

'Now mind,' old Auntie warned me, 'If thee dost get playin' about and lose me pension book I'll never let thee 'elp to scrape out me Nestle's milk tin agyn.'

It was an unnecessary caution; I had every intention of making a sedate bee-line down the rutted track to the post office-cum-shop at the bottom of our village. I intended to keep well to the forest side of the path to resist the distracting temptations of other children engaged in the ordinary pastime of playing. I was six years old and for the first time trusted alone for this very important mission.

I had old Auntie's livelihood in my pinny; her old age pension book from which she could draw five whole shillings a week. It was a fortune - even old Auntie thought so, and was apt to give as much praise to Lloyd George as she did to the Almighty for His munificence. She sang God's praises every

Sunday, and dratted the Devil for the rest of the week.

It was fair shares really, considering that a life of hard work, absolute honesty, and much kindness to others, had left her at seventy six years old a housebound arthritic with only enough savings put by to 'putt I under the ground dacent.' Rigidly independent of spirit, God knows how she would have managed had Lloyd George not come just in time with the five shillings a week old age allowance.

Fairly speaking, she could have accepted the little sustenance she required from us, for she had shared her home with Father from the day he had got married. We children had broken many of her treasured ornaments, kicked the legs off her best table, piddled on her feather beds, and trodden on her rheumaticky toes.

Mother had kept her lap filled with a succession of babies to be hushed and comforted to sleep. Father revered her, and we children adored her, this squared our books, for never by the slightest imputation did she make us feel indebted to her.

Too crippled to walk down to the post office to draw her pension herself, this task was entrusted to Father, and on this particular Friday afternoon I was going to meet him at the post office on his way home from his early shift at the pit.

Friday was a very special day for us children. It was pay day! However short work was at the pit

Mam always insisted Dad must have his shilling a week pocket money. Ninepence of this went on two packets of his beloved Stanfield tobacco, twopence on a slab of marzipan toffee for us children, and a penny on liquorice all-sorts for Mam and old Auntie.

Waiting outside the post office provided me with a lovely extra treat. In its little shop window was a shelf with a beautiful baby doll priced at half a crown. It had been there a very long time. Flanking the doll on each side was a doll's teaset in a car-board box, and a set of doll's furniture in another cardboard box, each priced at sevenpence. I was pleased no one could afford to buy them for it meant that I could 'pretend' play with them. Magic worked in those days. I 'got' them out of the window and sat down on the grassy bank outside to 'nurse' the doll, 'arrange' the furniture using little stones as substitutes, - then I pretend-drank my tea from the tiny cups, holding my little finger crooked in the manner my Aunties told me their mistresses did in service.

It was a wonderful treat too when I had Father's company all to myself. Father was a bottomless source of fascinating information, and all us children loved him to distraction. However, I got so engrossed playing with my pretend toys it was only when I noticed Father's mud-caked pit boots near me that I sprang up for my pit-grimed hugs.

I marched into the post office with him, my snub nose stuck even further into the air; after all we were cash customers with a whole shilling to spend!

When we got home Mam shared out the marzipan toffee, and magnanimously letting her have Dad's company I ran out to play - out into the beautiful green forest when school holidays and summer days lasted for ever. Yet winter came with its ills and chills, thinning us out with its icy brittle fingers, etching for ever on the memory a trail of black figures bent against the cruel snow-flecked east winds carrying a coffin in front of them, and the matching mourning of leaden skies, the creaking moans of dark leafless trees, and the black tread marks in the snow. That winter I came close to the edge of 'the pitty hole' myself.

Though by no means a particularly sunny-natured child, my persistent grizzling one evening attracted Father's notice before he went off to the night shift. He picked me up on his lap, felt my burning forehead, and noticed my heavy eyes and quickened breathing with some concern

'Mark my words thic young un be a' sickening fir zummat. The best place for 'er is bed an' a bit o' quiet.'

He put a brick to warm in the oven, helped Mam to make a bed for me in their room, and lit a fire in its tiny grate. When the fire had warmed the bed-room and the hot brick my bed, Mam gave me a washdown mustard bath, covered me with extra blankets borrowed from a kindly neighbour, and my worried father went out in the darkness to walk to the pit.

When he came home in the early hours of the morning I was worse.

Father's only culinary achievement was invalid's sop and he proceeded to make me some. He poured some boiling water on a piece of bread in a basin, beat it to a cream, adding sugar, a little knob of butter and a drop of milk. When my normally greedy little stomach refused to touch the delicacy, alarm set in.

Mam made some invalid drink - boiling water poured on a piece of toast and allowed to get cold. My siblings went to bed with hushed voices and tip-toe manner.

'I be goin' for the doctor' said Father.

For the doctor's and pride's sake two shillings off the arrears we owed him had to be multiple-borrowed from our impoverished neighbours, and Father ran through the woods to the doctor's house before going on his night shift.

Old Auntie, who have given up the struggle of getting upstairs to sleep, made a tortured ascent to sit with me whilst Mam did her evening chores and attended to the baby.

The doctor came, shook his head on my account, advised that the crisis would come shortly and my chance of surviving it was nil. His visit did not register on me: a black coma kept sucking me down. When I opened my eyes it was to unrecognisable surroundings. I could hear far away voices, and someone crying softly - 'I be afeared we be gwine to lose the little wench, Maggie, fir I never knowed anybody as bad as 'er is to get over it - and to think that only a couple 'o' days ago 'er was threadin' me needle for me as right as rain.' I could see no one, only weird terrible shadows on the wall and a pair of fiery tiger's eyes gleaming in the corner ready to pounce on me and eat me up. I must have screamed. Old Auntie pounded the floor with her walking stick, Mam rushed upstairs carrying the oil lamp. Some of the shadows disappeared, the tiger's eyes became the fire's reflection on the top caps of a pair of treasured boy's boots someone had given Mam for my little brother to grow into. Mam had kept them shined and polished on the bamboo what-not in the corner of the bedroom.

'Dad, Dad I want our Dad' I begged from this little oasis of lucidity. Dad would make the witches' shadows go, and the tigers save me from the black pit that kept sucking me down. Several times I struggled to consciousness to see Dad's face - but he was still down in his own black pit hacking on his knees for the coal that nearly kept our bodies and souls together.

'Dad, Dad oh I want our Dad' - and he was there - allowed straight up to the invalid's clean bedroom in his pit dirt. That dear kind face with the crinkles at the corner of his eyes, held my hands in his pit calloused ones. I was safe now. Dad was home.

'There there, my little wench, Faythers wum, an' I'll stop 'ere till thee bist better - now mind thees't got to make up thee mind to get better - for who's goin' to putt the taters in the dib 'oles for 'er old Dad, an' who's goin' to play wi' the babby whilst Mam do get on wi' the washin' - now thee take a sip o' thee Mam's drink and goo to a nice nap and I'll stop 'ere by thee bed.'

I took some spoonfuls from him whilst Mam fetched him up a cup of tea.

In the morning the doctor was amazed to find me still in the land of the living.

I had survived, but only just. I could make no headway with appetite or strength despite all the love and attention lavished upon me. My ten year old sister filled jars of flowers to put by my bed, Mam got little luxuries she couldn't afford to tempt my palate, but best of all I loved it when Dad came up to sit with me, to tell me stories or just to sit and read himself from one of the books a pit butty of his used to lend him.

One Friday, Dad came up with a cup and spoon in his hand and an expression of great pleading in his eyes. Beastly little daughter I must have been, for this was an ominous sign. Dad was a great believer in herbal medicines and often brewed his own from the herbs he gathered. I thought they tasted terrible and my pig-headed nature made me the most un-cooperative of swallowers, but I noticed what I thought was a book wrapped in brown paper in Dad's pocket. Perhaps Dad was going to sit with me for a long time.

With the patience of Job, and his own incredible gifts of love and encouragement, he got me to take eight spoonfuls of his little brew; then to bolster the undeserved praise he lavished upon me, he drank the dregs from the cup himself.

Then from his pocket he took the brown paper parcel, but it wasn't a book! He unwrapped it and put it on my bed. I could hardly believe my eyes. It was the box of doll's furniture out of the post office window!

'There then, that's fir bein' a good little wench. Now thee try and start yuttin' a bit better and then theel't be able to get up and goo out on the tump to play to thee 'earts content wi' all the tother young uns. Now afore I do go out to do a bit 'o' gyardening I'll 'a' me a little nap.' It was a little nap. As soon as he woke up it was always Father's habit to feel round for his beloved old pipe. He did so now, put it in his mouth, and then took his baccy tin out of his pocket. There was nothing in it. He put it and his pipe back in his pocket, then sat sadly staring through the window.

I remembered - today was Friday, pocket money day! Sevenpence for doll's furniture - twopence for marzipan toffee, a penny for liquorice allsorts - there was only twopence left!

I looked at my Dad, and I looked at my present, and I wished that doll's furniture was where old auntie sent the 'tarmenting devil,' all the way to Halifax.

The Rivals

They had been rivals in love. If 'Hell hath no fury like a woman scorned' it has no greater rivalry than when two females set their caps at the same man! In the case of Vernie and Lydie, whilst enjoying flattery of their attentions, the young man in question had been smart enough to escape his dilemma by marrying someone else altogether.

This mutual loss did not bring them together, each blamed the other, and though they eventually acquired a husband each they remained bitter enemies, ever trying to out do each other, especially in the matter of dress.

Both were talented needlewomen. Chapel anniversary was the highlight of their year and to outshine each other on that day was the summit of their ambitions.

Paris has its yearly bonanza of Haute Couture, and fifty odd years ago our chapel had its fashion parade too, on that important Sunday. Any girls lucky enough to be home from service on their annual holiday paraded the finery their hard earned shillings had bought them for the delectation of the village boys, but the 'starts' of the show were always Vernie and Lydie. Much to Lydie's chagrin, Vernie was always voted the winner. 'Wonder wot they two show offs 'll turn up in this time?' was a frequent conjecture of the village women who could not afford such indulgences.

At seven years old, ribbons and laces, frills and bows met with my undiluted approval, and a determination to indulge in them when I grew up and could earn some money. I was always happy when chance permitted me to sit on the corner of Vernie's fender and watch her sewing. Even her rag mats had a glamour. She didn't just poke the bits of rag through the sack at random; she patterned the colours and once earned a spate of childish praise from me when she fashioned a black cat in the middle of one from scraps cut from a dead old woman's skirt. But it was her drawers and chemises I especially envied; on the legs of the former she threaded pink ribbon through slotted borders and added frills of lace. Her washing day was 'a sight f'r sore eyes' as one man remarked - the women were not so charitable. 'I bet they never even go on 'er arse, 'er do just dip 'em in the wayter an' 'ang 'em on the line to show off.' No doubt the shape that Vernie possessed to fill them, that went with a very flirtatious pair of eyes in a pretty face, didn't endear her to them either!

Lydie also was no mean looker and she had the advantage of a crowning glory of naturally curly

auburn hair. Her luck however didn't last as far as
her legs. They were fat and shapeless, with ankles
that hung over the high heeled shoes she wore on
Sundays.

Having little sensitivity about how my 'social calls' were regarded, on occasions I took up my perch on Lydie's fender too, thus one summer becoming the innocent decoy of Vernie's underhand machinations.

'D'you know wot!' Vernie said to me one day a few weeks before Anniversary Sunday.

'D'you know wot' she repeated, her eyes shining, hands clasped together in apparent ecstatic anticipation - 'I be going to make meself a real classy dress f'r the anniversary, summat different, I be sick o' bright colours, I be goin' to wear black; a black velvut frock trimmed wi' black braid - I shall 'ave long sleeves to look different, an' a nice little close fittin' black 'at an' I shall wear me pearls, 'an very 'igh 'eeled black patunt shoes.'

I was rather less than enthusiastic at this description. I though black was the awfullest colour to wear and only fit for funerals.

Vernie enthused on - 'Wot made I think 'on't was a picture of a actress - on a postcard; 'er 'ad lovely ginger 'air and thic black frock 'er was wearin' set it off summat lovely. I read somewhere as well that all the smart 'igh up women be goin' in to black - they do reckon bright colours be too common. Oh I do wish I 'ad ginger wavy 'air, but I shall wear black just the same an' I'll bet I shall look smarter than all the t'others put together.

My hitherto unqualified admiration for Vernie's taste, plus here persuasive enthusiasm, nearly brainwashed me into thinking it a good idea; she went on so much about it I knew the details off by heart before my belly told me it was time to go home.

I had to go by Lydie's cottage further up the hill, near the chapel. I was passing her gate and got quite a surprise when she beckoned me inside from her doorstep.

'I've got a bit o' custard left in a basin if you'd like to yut it up?' Though my belly at that time was my god, and I took every opportunity to send it down an offering, it was ingrained in us village children not to accept from neighbours, who in general had pantries as bare as our own; but the temptation of custard, a rare treat for Sunday tea only in our house, and the fact that Lydie had no children to feed, and my scruples on this score gave in without a murmur. 'Come on, set down', Lydie said in a most kindly manner. She showed me a butterfly she was embroidering on a corner of a pillow case - the subject got round to sewing then to the Anniversary Sunday - then to the problem of what to wear for that grand occasion?

Without much prompting, and automatically imitating Vernie's fervent manner, I told her all about Vernie's plan to wear black. 'Vernie said - oo 'er wish 'er'd got ginger 'air cos then er'd look like that beautiful actress in the photo 'er got the idea from.' 'Ginger 'air like you got.' I added artlessly.

43

I had finished the custard, and was further astounded with a piece of bread and jam. Meantime Lydie skilfully got all the details of Vernie's forthcoming outfit from my mouthy chatter.

To augment the pittance they could get from their husbands meagre earnings - both Vernie and Lydie tramped the surrounding country in the autumn to earn their pins and needle money. They gathered acorns at 2d. a bucket under the forest oaks for a local pig keeper - and had their own blackberry territories. The 'Jam man' came in the evenings to the main road, at the bottom of the village with his horse and cart to buy this wild fruit. He was a proper Shylock; having no competition, he paid very stingily for his wares - he may not have got his pound of flesh but I reckon he got pints of blood from the scratches these two gathered in their pickings.

It was a perfect, very warm sunny Sunday on Anniversary day. Pretty outfits for me were still a figment of my imagination; meanwhile I must put up with whatever mother could muster for me to wear, being one of five children. No matter, I had my bit of glory to come; ever ready to show off, and blessed with a good memory, I was always given a 'spot' in the proceedings reciting a poem. We children who sang or recited sat on raised seats facing the congregation.

The chapel was soon packed, but the preacher, a local man well knew that two of his flock had not yet arrived, so he hung about in the pulpit. Vernie was hanging about too, crouched down behind her gate waiting to see Lydie emerge from hers. Lydie had been impatiently waiting for Vernie to go past. She looked at her clock - it was no good, she would have to start out.

Funereally garbed, hobbling painfully up the rain rutted path ('Like a pig on stilts' as Vernie gloated afterwards) - Lydie was hot, bothered and perspiring in her black velvet before she was half way to the chapel. When she was sure Lydie had got as far as the chapel door and the point of no return, Vernie started out.

What eyebrows I had shot up under my fringe when I saw Lydie hobble in and sink into the only vacant space at the back of the chapel. I thought she looked a miserable sight, and serve her right for copying Vernie's idea; for now the penny had dropped as well as the custard.

It was the turn of my big mouth next. It opened wide enough for all the trapped flies beating their wings against the chapel panes to come in for a flight, when Vernie made her entrance.

She was a vision in a cream silk sleeveless dress - a wide brimmed cream straw hat trimmed with a peachy pink rose and ribbons, cream dainty shoes, and crowning touch, a cream silk parasol, sprayed with roses to match the one on her hat! No black for her! The male organist had kept his seat right in the front row warm for her; he kept other things warm for her if local gossip was anything to go by.

Lydie's face went a quite dreadful red that clashed with her ginger hair, the look she gave Vernie's back view ought to have set fire to her rival and the one she gave me wasn't suitable at all for the chapel either!

Aches and Pains

When I was a child, as they aged, the old people in our village drew up their chairs nearer the fire, accepting their physical deterioration with a fatalistic stoicism, waiting for the Almighty to take them in His own good time. The doctors' pills and potions had not then superseded the powers of the Almighty. God and his angels were still up in the sky watching over them.

Sophisticated technology had not yet sent men soaring to the moon, destroying their comfortable illusions.

They still fought sickness with all the means at their disposal. Pneumonia might be cured with linseed meal poultices on the chest, - raw sheep's kidneys tied round the feet till the kidneys went putrid, drawing the poison out, - and boiled onion liquor to ease the throat. Often these 'cures', bolstered by love and encouragement, worked!

When the doctor diagnosed consumption, heads were shaken and the slow heartbreak began. When it was 'galloping consumption' the heartbreak came quicker.

Sonny Banes was only eighteen years old when the horrified whispers began to circulate that "im 'ad got it.'

The scourge could not have hit a less likely victim. Sonny had always been regarded as 'a regular caution,' a cheerful extrovert ready for any mischievous fun afoot. He brought rosy blushes to the girls' cheeks with his welcome ribaldry, and he was a very good looking boy too.

At 14 years old he cheerfully plodded to the pit in his heavy boots with the village men and other boys. A bit of 'chestiness' was so common his wasn't especially noticed. When opportunity gave Sonny the chance for a bit of idling underground the older men laughingly observed he was the exception to that old saying - 'One bwoy'll do one bwoys work - two bwoys together'll do 'alf a bwoys work - and dree bwoys together be nothin' but a 'indrance.'

His bouts of coughing and obvious exhaustion were put down to 'the bwoys outgrowin' 'is strength findin' 'is road to monhood,' When, however, the ebullient Sonny kept lagging behind them on the walk home ('me bloody boot laces be undone agyun') sympathy turned to alarm. 'Better take thic bwoy to the doctor f'r a tonic and 'av a check up missus,' they advised his widowed mother.

'I zid 'em comin' back dru the 'ood on their way wum from the doctor's, and thic 'oman was carryin' twenty more years on 'er shoulders than wot 'er started out wi"

The doctor had broken the news to Sonny's mother that he had the symptoms of advanced consumption.

She made him up his bed downstairs by the fire, fed him with the best at her disposal augmented by 'a bit o' this and a drap o' that' from sympathetic neighbours.

Poor Sonny's youthful contours dropped to skeletal proportions, but between his blood-flecked coughing bouts he was as cheerful as ever, flirting outrageously with any female from nine to ninety who popped in to see him.

He was fond of my father, who visited Sonny for a chat and a game of snakes and ladders whenever he could spare the time. One fine mild day Sonny made up his mind that he would come down to our house to visit father for a change, and he was determined to make it on his own; it was all of 300 yards. When Father heard this he got out our wooden chairs and asked some of the neighbours to place one every few yards for Sonny to have a rest. Then Father resisted the impulse to give the boy his arm - 'Let 'un come on 'is own if 'im can make it' he begged us.

Eventually Sonny got to the chair in our little courtyard. Mam poked the fire to a blaze under the kettle to give Sonny 'a nice 'ot cup o'tay' - and cut him a cheese sandwich from Dad's pit rations.

When he could get the strength, Sonny accepted the cup of tea placed on another chair near him. He was too weak to hold the cup for long - but he shook his head refusing the sandwich - 'it's a waste o'your victuals missus' he grinned, 'for 'tis no sooner in one end than 'tis out o' the tother. There's a pretty wench thee bist gettin'. (I wasn't, I was as plain as a pikestaff) Thee 'urry up an' get old enuff fr me to take thee to the pictures.'

Sonny couldn't stay long; Father walked behind him between his chair-rests and let him totter up unaided to his own cottage door.

Sonny never took me to the pictures. We never saw Sonny again. A week later his neighbour called asking if we could spare a couple of coppers towards a collection to help his mother with the funeral expenses.

Jarge

Normally, simple old Jarge was as placid and untemperamental as the sheep lying under the trees in the surrounding forest chewing their cud. After a few days of uncharacteristic grumpiness from the old man, one of his butties asked 'Wot's the matter old 'un? 'Ast thee bin gettin' out o' the wrong side o' the bed lately?'

One worthy who could have been a born medico in more affluent conditions hit the nail on the head with his diagnosis of Jarge's trouble.

"Ow long is it since thees't went to the mon 'ole old butty?'

The 'mon 'ole' was a natural hole in the forest, well hidden with surrounding undergrowth where the men went for nature's calls and left the bucket privies in the gardens for the use of women and children.

Jarge rubbed the stubble on his chin, and shook a negative head until enquiries had gone back a week.

'That's the trouble with thee old 'un; thee bist bunged up - I reckon a lump 'o' thy old 'omans bread pudding 'a' got stuck an' caunt't goo up or down - thee'lt vill up wi' gas like the cows do. Thee goo to the docter's tonight an' tell 'im thee bist constipated.'

Like most simple souls Jarge was apt to do what he was told. That evening he turned his muffler cleanest side out and walked the two miles to the doctor's surgery.

'And what is it that's troubling you, Mr. Dobbins?'
  'I be constipated, zir.'
  'I see, when did you last pass anything?'
  'On the road 'ere, zir.'
  'And what was it like?'
  'A 'oss an' cyart, zir.'

A bottle of senna mixture and a few sprints to the 'Mon 'ole' and old Jarge was chewing his twist of baccy again as contented as the sheep. He outlived the doctor, and when he was in his nineties the doctor's successor, by now an elderly man himself humorously suggested to the old man that the only way he could send him on his way was to shoot him!

A Bargain

When old Jarge had a couple of coppers to spare he toddled down to the pub at the bottom of the village, there to reflect on the vocabulary glory of his peers. He loved to pick up what he considered smart sayings to pepper his own limited conversation. When the two Wills' cousins were arguing about the selling and buying price of a young pig, Jarge was all ears.

'Dree pound I do want for thic' pig, and im's wuth every penny on't.'

'Two pounds ten I'll gi' thee, an im byunt wuth a grunt more.'

'Dree pounds.'

'Two pounds ten.'

'Dree pounds!'

'Two pounds ten!'

and on and on.

'Tell thee what then, I'll split the difference. Give I two pound fifteen.'

'Done.'

'Two 'alf pints o' zider, missus, and a charge 'em to thic Shylock,' demanded the seller.

Split the difference! Split the difference; the saying sounded very grand in old Jarge's ears. One evening sometime later, he went into the pub with a dead cockerel he had fattened up in the coop. It was a fine fat bird.

'I'll gi' thee one-and-six for thic 'un,' offered one of the men.

'I'll gi' thee one-and-nine fer'n,' said another.

'I'll make it two bob,' and the offers went on mounting up until the grand sum of half-a-crown waited for the hammer of Jarge's fist.

Blue eyes a twinkle with his own importance, chewing hard on his cud of tobacco, rubbing the grey stubble on his chin with the effort of getting his punch line in the right order round his tongue, old Jarge kept the last bidder waiting. Looking round his eager audience, and savouring his moments of drama, he brought his fist down hard enough to spill drops of cider from the glasses of the more parsimonious drinkers. Then Jarge got it out. 'Split the difference,' he boomed, 'Give I one-and-drippance.'

`Avin' a Goo

'Thee 'ave a goo old butty' - is the Foresters' way of expressing encouragement. Fifty-odd years ago, when I was a child, the lack of necessary skill did not deter a Forester from trying to help another in distress, even a bit of dentistry on one occasion!

One day when there was no work in the pit - Joe, Tim and Albert were squatting on the grassy slope outside Joe's house, when Dan lurched up, moaning and groaning and shaking his head from side to side. 'Wot's the matter old 'un?' 'The bloody jawache, that's wot's the matter, it be got that bad I'd be willin' for 'ern 'o' you to chop me yud off wi' a 'atchut.'

'That's a bugger that is, I've 'ad some on't in my time,' sympathised Joe - 'But I'll tell thee wot, if thee bist willin' I'll take thic tooth out for thee.'

'Ow?'

'Wi' me pinchers as I do castrate the animals wi'. Tim and Albert can 'old thee down, an' I'll pull on the bugger till 'im do come out. We wunt take no notice 'o' thee 'ollerin'; it'll be wuth the agony for to putt thee out 'o' such misery.'

Desperate, Dan agreed. With four hard knees on
the chest, and two pairs of pit-toughened arms
holding him down, and a mouthful of castrating

pinchers, Dan had little chance to get a holler out, but a cry of triumph came from Joe as he fell over backwards onto the grass.

'Thee'lt be alright now old butty; I 'a' got the bugger!'

His enthusiasm was not shared by the patient. Dan continued to roll his stricken head, and after poking about in his bloodied mouth, though grateful for the well meant intentions, he said sadly - 'my jaw do veel wurs than ever; I be afeared thee's took the wrong bugger out Joe.'

Big Ambitions

I could see my Aunty was nearly crying when she kissed us all goodbye before going back to her job in domestic service. All my five aunts who lived next door in Granny's cottage cried when their holidays came to an end. From what I heard them saying it was horrible being a servant. True they came home smelling all scenty, and powdered my nose with little pages from a paper powder booklet, and they got three-and-sixpence a week wages to buy pink silk stockings and pretty blouses, but I knew they would much rather be at home.

I was nearly five years old and was well aware that when I left school I too would have to go into service.

I hated the thought of leaving my mam and dad, and the family and our village, so I began to lay my own future plans.

I decided I would not go into service. I would go to work daily at the village pub, where I knew the landlady paid two shillings a week for doing the scrubbing and cleaning, with a bread and cheese dinner thrown in. I would live in Miss Phillip's cottage at the end of our garden. Miss Phillips was already old: she would have to be dead or go in the workhouse by the time I left school.

I loved babies, so I planned to have a dozen - six boys and six girls, all bastards - as I had heard the grown ups say. Bastards were very easy to come by, and I knew you didn't have to bother with a husband for that sort. I was puzzled why the women bothered with husbands, they were often so grumpy about them afterwards. I wouldn't mind one like my dad, but of course he was a very special sort of man, there wasn't another like him in the whole world.

I hated cheese, so I would bring home my cheese for the twelve babies and I could feed them on the forty-eight halfpenny ice creams my two shillings would buy. I kept my plans all to myself - until the day Miss Gabb called.

Mam was emptying the slops between the cabbages when she spotted Miss Gabb approaching our gate. Mam rushed in all in a tiz, taking off her sack apron, removing the nappies from the fireguard and the newspaper cloth from the table. 'Quick' she urged me 'Goo up to Mrs. Brown's and ask 'er if 'er can lend me a bit 'o' sugar - 'tis no good askin' Granny. 'Er'v' let me 'ave 'alf 'o' wot 'er's got in 'er sugar basin. Tell Mrs. Brown 'er shall 'ave it wi'out fail when our grocery do come tomorrow.'

Dear Mam, she loved to put the rare visitor a cup of tea, especially such a grand caller as Miss Gabb.

I put on my pig-headed, un-cooperative, bribe-demanding expression.

'If you can borrow me a bit 'o' sugar you can 'ave a suck 'o' the babby's sugar teat when 'ers gone.'

It was a bribe enough - Mam sometimes kept the baby quiet with a spoonful of dampened sugar tied in a piece of clean rag.

I got the sugar from kind Mrs. Brown and I had the gumption to take it into the back kitchen behind my back. I had long sensed that Mam did not like to advertise her poverty in these circumstances.

Miss Gabb was sitting by the fire, and I took up my perch on the corner of the big steel fender to give her one of my thorough optic going-overs.

How prim and neat she was, snow white blouse collar over her navy blue costume, hair drawn back into a tight little bun, and black shoes as shiny as brand new ones - all very suitable for a prudish middle-aged spinster who taught at Sunday School, had a preacher for her father and who was of independent means. She began to wilt a bit under my intense scrutiny and tried to break my concentration by asking me when would I be starting school and what I intended to do when I grew up. So I told her all about my twelve bastard babbys, my job at the pub and my intention not to be bothered with a husband.

She went very red in the face and slopped her tea into the saucer. Mam went red too; they didn't share my enthusiasm at all. Granny seemed quite pleased - I could see her trying to keep her mouth straight, and her soft child-rearing belly shaking under her pinny.

She cut off a lump of the bread pudding she had brought in as an excuse to be in on the tête-à-tête and 'cup 'o' tay.' Holding it in front of my nose like a carrot to a donkey, she got me outside.

"Ere you be, my wench, thees't better goo off to play with the t'others afore thees't put some o' thy ideas in Miss Gabb's yud, and I shouldn't hurry back if I was thee - I don't think thee mam's in a very good 'umour.'

I went down the path well pleased with my bread pudding, but very puzzled about the frequent oddness of grown-ups reactions to my bright ideas.

The Meeting

Only those too old, too ill, or too young did not come to the Meeting. People came from the outlying villages and hamlets to converge at the Hall, a plain oblong building used for the social activities of the community.

This particular evening it was not for pleasure - we wouldn't be laughing at Mr. Stott's comic recitations, or, come to that, the rather unappreciated singing of the grand local lady contralto.

We were going for a scolding - at least our dads, brothers, uncles, and granddads were, so it amounted to the same thing.

The menfolk were miners - miners who had dared to come out on strike rather than take a cut in their already pitifully inadequate wages.

Now the bosses and their managers were holding this meeting to remind these common, two-a-penny sparrows how grateful they should be for the crumbs thrown to them from the rich man's table. They were not a lot in number. As benefited their superior social and economic status, they sat on the stage looking down at their crowded, standing audience.

How marked was the contrast! Proper suits, starched white shirts, gold watch chains across well

filled bellies. Their ladies, grand in Sunday type hats, fur trimmed coats, well-shod feet and plump pink faces.

In the audience it was mufflers and caps, downtrodden boots, the gaunt grey underground faces of the men, and mostly pale undernourished faces of the women and children. Chesty coughs punctuated the waiting silence.

One of the men on the stage stood up - cleared his throat in an important sort of manner and advised the men to go back to work - or else. Time has dimmed his speech but not his pompous, condescending, down his nose attitude, but time has not dimmed the expression on my father's face as he listened to this rhetoric. Though Father was a great man in my eyes, physically he was a slight, pale-faced man, who had of late many extra holes in his leather belt to hold up his shabby trousers where his stomach should have been.

He looked at the speaker - then his eyes travelled round the audience - and the compassion in them, came, for want of another word, from what we call the soul.

Father was gifted with the sort of exceptional intelligence that made him a good man - a widely read man, a thinker, slow in his judgements and willing to see both sides of an argument, - and Father had made up his mind now which side he stood on.

The cruel economic systems geared to profit instead of human needs, man's foolish inhumanity to man culminating in wars and poverty - man's capacity for self destruction, was a burden he carried in his mind that often found him staring sadly into space. He had his blessings too - a great sense of wonder and appreciation for all the beauty that came his way, from the flora and fauna in the forest around us to the genius of artists, composers and scientists, to the very earth itself.

He waited until the speeches from the stage had finished. The downtrodden audience had sighed and coughed on, seeming visibly to shrink in their hopelessness. Then Father raised his hand to ask questions. Again the words are dimmed by time, but never their effect.

At first this upstart miner got some sarcastic comments - but quietly, Father continued to demand answer for question.

Soon their pomposity and bluster was pierced by his shafts of truth - it was they that began to look small - to squirm, to fidget, to get angry.

A change came over the audience. They had got a voice - an advocate the bosses had not the means to put down. Dull eyes shone, heads were lifted, shoulders squared to the world - they were men again, and as one man they called 'no' to their oppressors' demands. Belts would be pulled even tighter, for their future's sake women and children must suffer further, their backs were against the wall but now they had a pillow to support it.

During his seven-year victimization from the pits these men did not forget us.

Father was killed in the pit in 1945 aged 57 years.

He did not live to see the affluent miner, or the garage, car and bathroom a common-place in worker's homes, but I wonder if he were still alive, would he smile wryly to read as I did the other day that one percent of the population still have control of eighty percent of the nation's wealth!

Entrance and Departure

In our village, life was simple and 'near the knuckle,' food for an extra mouth was hard to come by, yet it could not diminish the glory of each new birth.

The stairs to the bedroom might be only of scrubbed wood, but the new father (perhaps too many times over), would tip toe up them reverently to marvel at the tiny fingers he could curl around one of his pit calloused ones.

'Well done my wench, that's a little beauty thees't got there!' would be thanks enough for the tired face on the pillow.

However long the black angel hovered, the deaths of even the oldest inhabitants got their share of sighs and tears.

'I be afeared 'er time be come' the bed-watchers whispered out of hearing of old Ginny, when the indomitable old woman could no longer infuse strength of her spirit into her worn out body, and took to her bed.

Resigned at last, she saved her gasping breath to talk over old times with the old faces still around her. There was no need to dip into the carefully hoarded

pittance, saved 'to putt I down dacent,' for a doctor's
diagnosis.

'We'd better get Edie Paine to come and 'ave a look
at 'er; thic 'oman can see death in anybody's eyes as
soon as it be knockin' on the door.'

'Ay. An 'er can see by a 'oman's eyes when a babby is on the way, sometimes afore the 'oman be sure of it 'erself.'

Edie Paine, widow, washerwoman, midwife and layer-out of the dead, dispenser of goose grease for the chest, herb teas for the colic, and a trusted friendly ear for private troubles. When called she went to old Ginny's bedside.

Honest kindly eyes looked into honest eyes.

'I do know wot thee bist come for Edie, but I ben't quite ready for thee yet.'

The soapy-water-wrinkled hands took the emaciated geriatric ones in hers for a warm goodbye.

'Sometime between midnight and six o'clock' Edie advised the neighbours who accompanied her to the door.

Old Ginny didn't let her down. Just after 4 a.m. she gave up watching the flickering candle on the washstand and let the darkness come.

Conscience Stricken

Big eared, chopsy, and tactless, with a penchant for letting cats out of bags, and for exposing the skeletons in the family cupboard, I was the sort of child mothers like out of the way when visitors are around. However, this was a special occasion and mother was determined to show her brood off.

By our terms this visitor was a proper somebody. I had learned that he was elderly, a lay preacher, who had settled many years ago in Yorkshire after leaving our impoverished mining village to look for work. He had made himself 'a tidy bit o' money' keeping a grocery shop up there, and, most important to a mercenary little six year old, 'There might be summat in it for you if you be a good little wench,'

'Summat' might mean a toffee, two toffees! A halfpenny!! Or even a penny!!! My optimism travelled like a kangaroo by leaps and bounds. I decided it was worth co-operating with Mam. It was quite a trial; it meant giving in without a struggle to having my knees washed as well as face and hands, the tangles combed out of my hair, the responsibility of a clean pinny, and worst of all, sitting still and keeping my mouth shut. Strictly speaking he wasn't

really our visitor at all; he was coming to see our aged great-aunt with whom we lived.

Old Auntie who was chair ridden with arthritis didn't have to have her knees washed; no one could see them under her long black skirts, but we brought her a wet flannel and towel for her face, Mam tied her on a clean pinny and brushed her sparse strands of white hair into a tidier little bun, assuring her that she looked 'quite respectable.'

The freshly nappied baby lay on the sofa contentedly sucking his sugar teat, Mam kept rubbing over the big blackleaded grate until it shone. We youngsters tried to be as still and as wooden as the chairs we sat on. It was purgatory, but after one of Mam's quick peeps outside, she dramatically hissed at us that "im was a comin' down the garden path.'

He took his time, for he was quite old. When he came in I thought he looked like a cross between Methuselah and one of the Disciples. He had white hair and a long white beard, watery blue eyes below bushy white eyebrows, puffed pinky cheeks and a moist pink mouth I didn't take to at all. It wasn't his physiognomy I was particularly interested in; it was in listening for the crackle of a sweet packet or the chink of coins in his pockets. He looked affluent enough for both; in a black suit grand enough for funerals, starched white shirt and gold watchchain shining across his chest. Mam pulled up the other best chair with arms on nearer the fire opposite old Auntie's. They took an interminable time reckoning up the dead and gone, and recalling old times, before Mam's polite coughs got a bit apprehensive regarding our forbearance, but at last he turned his attention to us.

The baby got a short nursing on his lap, spent a penny in the form of a big wet patch on the visitors knee and made a profit of twopence by getting a silver threepenny-bit put in his hand. The omens were good! My little brother next. He was soon off his perch having tried hard to pull the old man's beard off. I decided he was like a Disciple for he still gave my brother a penny. I was a bit worried, though, about this sort of financial index - there was still a little sister to come before me. She was a pretty, quiet, fair little creature and sat long enough to absorb most of the damp patch and she too got a penny. My evaporating patience returned. At six years he considered me eligible for a sermon; advising me that if I said my prayers every night, attended Sunday School regularly, and never disobeyed my elders, I should go to Heaven when I died. I wasn't struck with this bargain - we had texts and pictures of angels hanging around the walls upstairs and I had come to the conclusion being an angel was very boring; just floating around in the sky all the time. I preferred it on earth, where I could get broken bits of china and rusty tins off the ashmix to play shops with, and make houses out of the lush green ferns under the trees, and only get a smack if Mam could catch me when I was naughty instead of going to Hell. However I didn't aim to risk a possible penny by correcting him, and at last, I got one, and I knew just what I was going to spend it on, - lucky, lucky me! Oh! What a lovely day it was! I was up our garden path like a rocket.

As far as I was aware there was only one cherry tree in the world, and it was in Prudence the witch's garden, the cottage below ours. Many a dribble had gone down the front of my pinny longing for some of the luscious ripe cherries on it. Now I could buy a whole pennyworth and hide down in our empty pigs-cot for a feast.

We reckoned Prudence was a witch because she never wanted to mix with the rest of the village, and had a nasty habit of crouching down behind her gate in the dusk - popping up like a jack-in-the-box making a weird crackling laugh if a child went by. She could perform miracles too, because all the women said it was a miracle where Prudence's son had come from. She hadn't got a husband, was never seen ever talking to a man and the village women seemed very annoyed wondering where she had got him. He was quite big and strong but not quite all there in his attic - but he was very good at shinning up the cherry tree to pick the wares. We forgot about her being a witch when her cherries were ripe!

I was stopped in my tracks when I reached our garden gate by a most unusual sight! A beggar women, in our village! I had heard about beggars, and how sometimes they had gold sovereigns hidden under their ragged clothes. Perhaps that was the reason no one came out of our penny-pinched community to give her anything. Apparently it was against the law to actually knock on the doors to beg - so this old woman was supposedly singing for her supper - I thought she sounded worse than a cat on the tiles and anyway it was cherries, not charity, that occupied my mind. I ran down to Prudence's door and soon got a nice lot of cherries in a piece of newspaper. I didn't have to share with my siblings, they had all got their own money, so clutching my precious hoard I made my way back to our gate en route for the pigs-cot.

I wasn't pleased to see Dilys Pugh leaning up against it. She was a few years older than me - a 'stuck up,' well dressed, only child with a caste system of her own. She regarded me as one of the head scratching, droopy-drawered, inferior untouchables.

She had a long nose and plenty of practice looking down it. She was a born scolder, worse than a governess at school, and kept showing off by pulling her proper hemmed handkerchief out of the legs of her drawers even when her nose didn't need wiping.

If you said 'bugger' when a sharp stone went up through the hole in your boot sole she was so shocked she told your mam and probably got you a good hiding. I had no intention of offering her any cherries.

'I'll tell your mam if you yut any on 'em' she warned me.

'I don't care, they be mine anyroads.'
'Pooh, don't tell lies you've got a pennoth there and the likes o' your mam can't give a penny fir yourself.'

'It bent lies, we got a visitor, and 'im gid the lot on us a penny, an "im gid the babby drippunce, so there!'

Dilys pulled herself up to a bit above her normal height, pursed her lips to a thinner narrower line, took a deep breath through flared nostrils that swelled out her narrow chest. She looked at me with her 'God help them for they know not what they do' expression. Her eyes concentrated into accusing slits. I thought she was going to explode.

'Dost thee mean to tell I that thees't spent a whole penny on thee own greed guts with thic pore old varmint up there a tryin' to sing 'er 'eart out to get some money fir summat to yut! - 'ers likely to drop down dyud afore long from starvation - the trouble with thee, theest got no conscience, I'll bet thees't 'ad some dinner today, not like thic pore old creature.'

I looked at the old woman again with 'seeing' eyes. Oh how pitiful she was, so skinny, so raggedly dressed. I remembered my dinner; Mam had made a big suety pudding and put a good sprinkling of sugar over it. Oh! What a thoughtless wicked greedy girl I was! If only I could get my penny back, but I didn't dare ask Prudence such a thing. Never mind, I would give the old beggar woman my untouched cherries. I ran up to her and thrust them in her hands. To my intense surprise and disappointment she didn't seem at all pleased. She put them away somewhere in the folds of her ragged skirts without even a thank you or a smile. I staggered back against a garden wall and started to walk down to Dilys who had been watching. Dilys too appeared to have lost interest; she turned and went on her way down the village. I stood by our gate; I had no penny, no cherries, not even a thank-you.

I was square with my conscience but it brought little comfort - I decided there and then that me and my conscience didn't get on very well together.

A Loss

There was a proper midwife who wore a navy blue bonnet tied under her chin, a navy cape, and carried the bag 'she brought the babies in.' Most of the women managed with the village midwife, a skilled, kindly, self-taught woman who took a mere pittance for her services, and was the soul of discretion regarding the lack of sheets and other necessities for the confinement. She often added the bonus of bowls of her gruel and pieces of clean white rags for the new mother to hem napkins whilst she stayed the statutory ten days in bed.

The village midwife, the proper nurse and the doctor were called in on one occasion but between them all they could save neither mother nor child.

Letty was a bonny young wife who had carried her first pregnancy right up until the ninth month as easily as she carried her bundles of kindling wood home from the forest. By then her neat slim little figure had such a dimensional preponderance folk laughingly observed it would be bound to be twins there, if not triplets! There were no clinics for the measuring of pelvic bones, urine tests or the other safeguards now in practice. Only the wise village midwife felt alarm for Letty. When the girl's labour

started, before it got too protracted she sent the young husband for the proper midwife. The professional midwife had no wish to diminish her own status by calling in the doctor, but after many hours she relented and the fleetest footed teenager in the village was sent running the two miles for the doctor.

The worried, bewildered young husband was reluctantly made to go to his shift at the pit by the midwife. 'You'll do no good here - just be in the way, and with another mouth on the way to feed you can't afford to miss your work.'

He put his feet towards the pit but his head kept turning back to the cottage window where Letty suffered in the big iron bedstead. Before he reached the pithead she had bent the iron bed head in the mad agony of her turmoil.

The good old doctor was away on an urgent case of pneumonia - but the boy left the message for him to visit. By the time his horse and trap drew up at her cottage gate - Letty's eyes were glazing over, and her knuckles were bitten to the bone in her suffering. The doctor knew this child would never be born. Not for the first time he cursed nature and its methods of reproduction. The nearest hospital then was eighteen miles away, and transport a horse and cart. He knew the girl would not survive the journey. He had not the skill, the means, or the trained help to perform the necessary caesarean operation in a primitive cottage bedroom. He had only laudanum and it was getting too late for that, but youth dies hard.

The village midwife, stricken by the turn of events, asked the weeping neighbours to send a couple of men to way-lay the young husband, now on his way home from the pit. 'Tell 'em to kip 'im away from 'ere somehow - tis better 'er be gone than 'im should see the wench like this.'

Sick in their hearts two men hurried off through the woods trying to think up a ploy to keep the young man out of earshot of his cottage. He saw through their false cheer and hindrance. Sensing a conspiracy and full of foreboding, he broke from the physical constraint they were forced to use. He rushed indoors and up the stairs and watched his sweetheart wife die.

The women wept and said 'I shall 'ear thic poor wenches screams till the day I die.' Men hung their heads in sorrow - 'This pore bwoy, 'im'll be like a young tater that 'a' bin nipped by a black frost - im'll never be the same agyun.' The young man never was the same, he never married, he relinquished his manhood. 'I'd never do anything that 'ud putt a 'oman dru that agyun.'

We children knew him as a kindly, eccentric, white-haired old man, who looked at us with tender rheumy eyes. Perhaps we were all like living ghosts to him, ghosts of the child he never had.

A Good Clane Out

Facts are facts and have to be faced, and in truth when I was a little girl, next to my Dad, I loved my belly. It was a tyrant always sending messages up for any thing I could scrounge for it. I was a good scrounger, from old great auntie's bacon rinds and crusts, too hard for her toothless gums to chew, to the bits of corn I could pick up before Miss Philips' fowls gobbled them when she threw a couple of handfuls to them over her garden gate. Best of all, my stomach and I mutually agreed, was suet treacle pud and Granny was our greatest benefactor in this respect. Granny's bevy of daughters were all away in domestic service or married; only her son remained at home, but Granny never made suet pud for just the three of them. She waited until she could get enough ingredients for her household, our household and any other children within sniffing distance. Pudding cloths were her problem. Clean white rag was hard to come by and there were so many other uses for it. Babies' bums for instance and there were plenty of them about!

Granny's problem was solved on one occasion when one of her daughters brought home from service a couple of white cotton tennis stockings given her by her mistress. Just the job, thought Granny!

Granny mixed her puddings in her huge bread crock, then stuffed them by the yard down the stockings. She filled her copper with water and lit the fire underneath it. When she finished her washing, it was Granny's habit to rinse the copper out with clean water and soap, and dry it. Something must have distracted her on the previous washday, for a residue gel of Hudson's Powder and soap had been left in the bottom. Now, Granny's copper was in the darkest end of her dark little kitchen, at the back of her cottage. Unaware of the soap, when the copper came to the boil the clouds of steam hid the frothy water and Granny couldn't smell it. She had lost her sense of smell from a severe sinus illness years before. The puddings bubbled about like a bunch of anaemic Loch Ness Monsters.

We children and our friends stayed near at hand playing hopscotch on the piece of hard trodden earth outside our garden gate, - waiting, - waiting for Granny's calls.

At last - 'Come on in me butties, bring summat wi' yer to putt yer puddin' on.'

We lined up with our saucers etcetera by her back kitchen door, taking our turn by her salting slab for our dollop of pudding and ration of warmed treacle. Then we perched in tiers on the stone steps leading from her garden down to her tiny courtyard, just in case a second helping might be forthcoming.

A second helping! We could hardly down the first!

Something had gone amiss; the pudding tasted bitter and soapy. We were no gourmets, and the anticipation had been so great, besides, we were well mannered enough to hide our disappointment from our beloved Granny. We controlled our grimaces of distaste and swallowed every mouthful.

Granny always left herself till last, but there was some in the toe of one of the stockings for her.

Life hadn't made Granny a gourmet either, but she pulled a very wry face with her first spoonful, then realising what she had done, she said, 'Laird 'o' merssy this puddin' be awful - Oh my gawd I 'ope I 'an't pizened the lot on you - oh well, if I 'ave I might as well pizen mezelf too" - and she ate hers all up as well.

The stomach spasms didn't hit us all at once - but it was frequently one-in-and-one-to-go doubled up outside the garden bucket-privvy.

However black the clouds gathered on Granny's horizon she always poked in them for a bit of silver lining. She found some then.

'I'll tell thee what,' she observed to mam, - 'thee 'outn't need to give any of 'em doses 'o' brimstone and treacle f'r a bit - I reckon all their insides 'ave 'ad a good clane out.'

A couple of years later Granny moved to another part of the Forest. We missed her even more than her treacle puddings. Through Granny's eyes the world was an infinitely richer place. When I was a young married woman of twenty-six and visiting my parents, Granny walked through the woods the two-and-a-half miles to us for a 'squat an' a chat.'

When it was time for her to go I walked most of the way back with her. We stopped for a breather in a little valley with steep wooded sides. It was so peaceful and beautiful there; a sparkling little stream meandered through beds of watercress, birds sweetly twittered in the branches over our heads; the dappled sunshine through the trees gave a perfect mixture of warmth and shade and the moss covered earth was soft beneath our feet.

Granny stood there for some minutes quietly gazing around, then she sighed - 'ah, my wench, I mustn't grumble, the Almighty 'a' bin good to me, f'r 'im a let me goo past me dree score years and ten, and the time be comin' soon f'r me to goo - but oh my wench I shall miss all this!'

Now I am getting old, dear Granny, I know just how you felt.

Dashed Hopes

I'll tell you what to do, Maggie.' Granny's voice was low, urgent and conspiratorial. 'We'll make up some pizen – we can make it out o' some deadly nightshade – then if thic Kaiser gets 'is armies over 'ere and they come anywhere near us - we'll pizen the little uns fust, then take zum ourselves – I'll never let them varmints put they dear little young uns on the end 'o their bayonets.'

I knew I was one of 'them dear little uns' Granny was talking about. It was 1917. I was three years old – and I knew there was something called a war on – It was all the fault of a wicked man called Kaiser who lived in a country named Germany and was sending his armies into England to kill us all off and have it for himself. The war – the war – everyone, especially women, kept on talking about it – but I could see no sign of it anywhere. Old Great-Auntie, sitting in the chair nearest the fire, was fast asleep, her toothless mouth agape – she didn't seem worried. It was a comfort. I had never seen a soldier – the men in our village were all miners and exempt from call-up. Coal, and more coal, was needed, all the coal that could be got to stoke the fires of this man-made hell on earth.

It was lovely when Father was home from the pit and I could take my turn with the others for a sit on his lap. Then I felt safe and secure from the Kaiser , from the war, from the shadows on the wall, even from the thunder and lightning that sent Mam cowering in the coalhole under the stairs. Granny often came into our house from next door. Granny couldn't read herself, but she brought Grancher's paper in for Mam to read. She, old Auntie and Mam would cuddle us round the fire while Mam read all the awful news from the war front, news exacerbated by all the ghoulish rumours about the wicked Germans. Father had no patience with these sessions.

'Them Germans be no different to we lot or any other country – them soldiers over there do as them be told the same as our lot. They be no more responsible for this war than we be – and you women do want your yuds examined if you do swallow all you read in the papers, or what do get about on people's tongues. 'Twas the Boers last time – and when this lot's over, after a bit, another war'll break out somewhere else. We 'uman bein's be supposed to have brains but we be wuss than the animals. The world's a sick place – all us 'ave bin from what I've read, and all us will be till they got enough sense to share things instead o' fightin' over 'em, and they've got more gumption than you dree swallowin' everything you be told.'

Such conversations were beyond my comprehension, but even at that age Father had an aura for me that made me his ally.

The war came into our house with the grocery man. Miners were now earning enough to keep their families' bellies well filled, but rationing kept us short. Old Auntie got a precious ounce of butter – she loved her 'bit o' best butter.' When it went missing off the table one day the house was in turmoil. Mam and she had definitely seen it when the grocer had delivered it along with Auntie's three-cornered blue paper bag of sugar, a tin of Nestle's milk, bit of redrinded cheese, etc. How could it have vanished into thin air? I had been playing with a neighbour's toddler son indoors; my mouth was inspected inside and out, and my small person thoroughly frisked for evidence – despite my denial of crime.

Only when our neighbour undressed her little boy for bed did she find the bit of greasy paper in his pocket and the oily stain on his trousers. This little tragedy was recounted for weeks.

I knew the war had ended when Granny came in and picked us up one at a time and did a dance in our tiny courtyard. Old Auntie kept thanking the Almighty for his deliverance. I almost stopped worrying about the Kaiser coming to kill me in the night. The need for coal slackened down – gradually the men were put on short time, especially when coal was imported from the Saar as reparation from the beaten enemy. Rationing finished, but our grocery deliveries didn't improve all that much.

At five I started school. On winter evenings, perched on the end of our steel fender, I often listened to Father and his pit butties talking. Their talk ranged on many subjects – war was one of them. I knew that the subject of war particularly saddened and angered Father. I sensed that he might be worried lest my little brother go to war when he grew up.

One evening when I was about eight years old, Father came in from a meeting. He had a book in his hand, his face was white and taut. Granny, Old Auntie and Mam were sitting around the fire.

'Here,' said father to them. 'Take a look at this book, than you'll see what war is all about.'

I could see the title of the book was *War Against War,* but I was not allowed to look inside. I knew where Father put the books he thought unsuitable for childish eyes – on top of the cupboard by the fireplace. I waited my opportunity to climb up on a chair when no one was about. I turned over the pages and became a pacifist for life.

Here was proof of a man's bestiality to man – if his capacity for evil was exploited. No wonder Father worried. I could not comfort him or go to him for comfort. I had disobeyed him getting up on the cupboard. The dread of war, though often forgotten in happy playing, hung over my childish head.

A quarter of an hour before school, prayers for the end of lessons one day, our teacher told us to put away our composition books because she had something to tell us. As she spoke the sky grew a more fairy blue through the windows, the flowers in the jam-pots on the window-sills more exquisite, and her pleasant face with its aura of fair hair began to look like an angel's, for she was telling us about something called the League of Nations – about the treaty the leaders of these nations had signed to prevent another war.

No dawdling home from school for me that day – no joyous runs into the ferns from the woodland path. No linking arms with the other girls, whilst singing our favourite school songs – I was the bearer of magic news – weighed down not at all by my black leather studded boots.

'Where's our dad?' I demanded breathlessly of Mam.

Down in his shed – wot's up?'
I couldn't stop to tell her. Father was in his little shed at the bottom of the garden. He was quite a handyman. Here he mended our boots, did a bit of amateur carpentry, and soldered his and his pit

butties' carbide lamps. It was mostly an honorary pastime – there was often no money to pay for his services. He had fashioned his own brazier from a large round tin with a fire-bellows fixed in the side to heat the soldering iron white-hot. I loved to watch Father soldering. The tiny balls of liquid metal needed such a delicate touch to spread it on the cracks in the metal lamps with the soldering iron. It was not a time for distractions – but my wonderful news cast such considerations aside.

'Dad! Dad! There ben't goin' to be any more wars!' He went on with his soldering. My words could not have sunk in. I tugged at his sleeve. 'Dad! Dad! Did you 'ear wot I said? – there ben't goin' to be any more wars!'

'And wot makes you think that, my wench?'

'Our teacher told us, Dad. A lot of countries 'ave done summat called the League o' Nations. They've signed a treaty so there won't be any more wars.'

Father lifted me up on his work-bench. He looked through the window with sad faraway eyes.

'I be afeared, my wench, that this treaty by un't wuth the paper 'tis wrote on.'

My spirits sank down in my heavy boots – but I had grown never to doubt the truth or wisdom of Father's words. As simply as he could, he explained to me about the moving balances of the world trade – about the discoveries of natural resources and how, even by going to war, nations sought to obtain the lion's share of these things. He told me about man's ego patriotism, and ego religions, about all the things that made them enemies.

My stricken face must have disturbed him. 'There, there, my wench, Father shouldn't 'a' worried thy young yud wi' such talk. Doesn't thee worry, there

94

may never be a war in thy time. I'll tell thee what — I 'a' got a nice bit o' rope 'ere, and two pieces o' wood that'll do for handles. Thee goo and ex thee mother to wet I a cup o' tay and I'll make thee a skippin' rope.'

I have lived through a Second World War — the powers of East and West threaten each other with the atom bombs — somewhere or other a war is always going on on this earth. Unlike Granny, Mam and Old Auntie, I never believe all I read in the papers.

Kezzie

Because she was such a bright little scholar, our exasperated teachers often overlooked some of Kezzie Larkin's shortcoming, for Kezzie was a bit of a handful.

The cottage 'over on the Green' where the Larkins lived was looked down on by villagers. It was overrun with little Larkins; 'nothin' but a bloody rabbut warren', was how one man described it.

Kezzie was the eldest of six children. Despite her ragged clothes, tangled nitty hair and dirt-engrained knees, Kezzie had enough charisma to be accepted by the rest of us. God knows we village children had absolutely no grounds to be toffee-nosed about anyone, but children, of course, form their own hierarchies just as grown-ups do. In our childish eyes, pretty girls were those lucky enough to have be-ribboned curls and tidy clothes; looks and form had nothing to do with it.

Grown-ups were more observant. I remember one man remarking to another as they watched us at play:

'I doubt thee'lt ever clap thee eyes on a purtier wench than thic young Kezzie. I bet the kings o' England 'ould give zummat to 'ave daughters as looked like thic little wench.'

Recalling Kezzie in my mind's eye, I see a thin little face with a pair of long-lashed, expressive eyes, flecked with green and hazel, a neat small, straight nose and a mouth that rarely turned down at the corners. My eldest sister and Kezzie were the two top scholars in their class.

Kezzie was the younger by six months, but they were close chums. Kezzie knew where the rain made puddles for illicit paddling, where the best wild strawberries grew, and the right places to go scrumping apples. She organized us into 'concert parties', performed acrobatics like a monkey from tree branches, and could make up the most exciting fibs to scare us out of our wits. Her skinny, muscle-knotted arms packed a terrific punch in defence of her tribe of small brothers. Carrying no ballast, she could run like the wind, leading us to safety when pursued for our misdemeanours.

The Larkins' fecundity was a sore problem to many of the village women; they were full of sympathy when rumour had it that Kezzie's mam was 'in the cyart aygun'.

"Tis a cryin' shame, there's more mouths over there already than victuals to put in 'em.'

Mrs Larkin had her baby, a girl this time.

The words, 'Gone to a better place,' seemed only too true when the news got around six weeks later that the baby had died. Mrs Larkin was in a bad way too, hardly able to walk, with swollen, ulcerated legs.

As it neared chapel treat time I stepped up my attendances at Sunday School to get enough marks for this special day of the year. The kindly old man who took Bible class asked Gladys, Dolly, Lil and me if we would be four little Christians and act as pallbearers to carry the baby to church. There would be no mourners and no service inside the church because the baby had not been christened. The mother was too ill to go but the vicar was willing to say a few words before she was buried in some unconsecrated ground at the back of the churchyard. We were eleven years old – too young for any depth of feeling, but we felt very sombre and important as we looked at each other for assent and nodded. 'Yes.'

All our mams picked us a little bunch of flowers to go on the coffin and Lil's mam made us a black armband each to wear.

It was a lovely warm sunny day, a day to shin up trees, scamper in and out of the ferns beneath them, and jump for joy over the huge oak-roots exposed across the woodland paths, but we felt the solemnity of the occasion and walked sedately, remembering all the miserable things we could talk about. It would be cruel to the dead baby to be cheerful.

I had never been in Kezzie's house before; I was shocked. I thought our house was a palace in comparison. Our Mam made rag-rugs to put in front of the grate; we had a pair of brass candlesticks and a vase on our mantel-piece; our Dad had made some shelves for Mam to show off the cups, saucers and plates she had got with her tea coupons. Here there was only an old sack on the floor, the bits of lace curtains had more holes than lace, not an ornament anywhere, and the tables and chairs looked very kicked about.

The little home-made coffin was on the table. Mrs Larkin, who looked very ill, hobbled over to it, I could see her swollen ankles all ulcerated and bleeding … she lifted the lid of the coffin. I had been privately of the opinion that new babies looked little different to skinned rabbits, but this one looked like a white marble doll, paler than the nightdress she was laid out in. The Larkins had to lug the water much farther than the villagers from the communal well. A little posy of wild flowers had been placed between

98

the baby's hands. Two tears from Mrs Larkin's eyes bedewed them as she kissed the baby goodbye. There was pride as well as grief in her voice as she called on us to witness what a little angel her baby looked.

The lid was fastened down, two ropes were tied round with loops for carrying, and we started out. Mrs Larkin picked a toddler up from the floor, rocking him in her arms for comfort. A couple of her other little boys followed us as far as the well. 'Where's your Kezzie gone?' Lil asked them.

'Nowhere – 'er ben't gone nowhere – 'er's zittin' round the back o' the 'ouse wi' 'er pinny over 'er yud a cryin'.'

It was a mile to the church. We kept to the grass verge of the main road. Only one timber wagon passed us, cars were still a rare sight in those days.

The vicar stood in the church porch. He met us outside while a man stood in the open grave to let the coffin down. The vicar mumbled a few words and led us out of the churchyard.

'Don't worry,' he said, 'I'm sure the Good Shepherd will take this little lamb into His flock.'

When we were out of earshot Lil observed rather tartly, 'Of course that babby'll goo to 'eaven. All babbies do 'cos they 'an't done nothin' wrong.' We felt quite comforted.

We didn't go back to the Larkins' house; we knew there would be no funeral meats – not even a cup of tea to spare.

By the winter all the village was in similar straits to the Larkins. Our dads – all miners – had come out on strike rather than submit to even worse conditions than they had already endured in the cruel economic climate of the twenties. It was an awful struggle for our mams to get something for us to take to school for our mid-day break.

Our Mam had melted some mutton fat down for dripping spreading it on bread whilst it was still warm. It had re-congealed into hard white lumps but was going down sweet enough until our young noses sniffed the unfamiliar odour of meat. *Meat!* Who could possibly be eating meat?

We were allowed to sit in the main classroom for our lunch-break. The whispers came back up the row of desks.

'It was they Larkins lot *yuttin' meat.'* No bread, they hadn't got any bread. 'Just girt chunks o' lean *meat.'* It was astounding information. And they kept bringing meat day after day.

Then one day none of the Larkins came to school and the rumour got around that the police had taken Mr Larkin away. He had been sheep stealing. Fifty years before he would probably have been hanged for the crime. Instead he was summonsed – sent to jail – and the bailiffs called in to sell up his household goods towards recompense for the sheep-owners.

'Poor bugger, I'd a done the zame livin' up there out o' sight with me young uns starvin'. They baillies got to leave the beds; it's the law: they mustn't sell the beds.'

We were as a rule ready gawpers at anything outside the common rut – funerals and weddings. A cat stranded up a tree, a harangue between neighbours, the odd drunk – all got our rapt attention.

But with no means to help the Larkins, no one from the village had the heart to go and watch.

'Their veow sticks o' farniture zold over their yuds: I doubt the lot put together'll vetch a couple o' quid.'

'Poor devils. It'll be the work-house for 'em now.'

Children and mothers were segregated in the work-house; her children were all that Mrs Larkin had left.

''Ave you 'eard about the Larkins? They've gone in wi' the gypsies.'

'Never.'

''Tis right enough. Our Tom was walkin' dru the wood by the gypsies' camp and 'im zid the Larkins boys a playin' wi' the gypsy young uns and 'im could zee a iron bedstead in one o' the tents.'

The strike was over, the beaten men went back to work, but not our Dad. There was no job for him. He was labelled a radical upstart because he had openly spoken up against the oppressors. He tramped the days away looking for work, but a day's work of any sort was almost impossible to come by. His pit coal allowance was gone, but we drew our chairs up to a good fire that winter. Buckets of coal were tipped inside our garden gate, and there were kindling wood to be gathered in the surrounding forest.

One bitterly cold night, a cruel east wind, full of icy sleet, beat against our window and blew the piece of sacking away put to stop the draught coming under the door.

'I wonder 'ow they poor little Larkins young uns be standin' this out in them tents in the 'ood,' said Mam sadly. I shivered in sympathy, soon forgotten as I cuddled with my siblings under Mam's heavy home-made patch-work quilts. We survived the winter, spring came to cheer us up, then summer and a day of great anticipation. After a year in service our sister was coming home for her annual holiday. We didn't know what time. Dad was in the back kitchen shaving and Mam was polishing over the blackleaded grate for the umpteenth time when a neighbour came puffing down our garden to tell us she couldn't be sure, but somebody was comin' up the village that might be her!

Dad wiped the lather off his face and ran through the door – his face naked with the love for this treasured home-comer. I saw him take her into his arms through the window. How could this glamorous, beautiful young woman be our sister?

I thought she had been dressed up to the nines when she left home in her new navy serge dress and black shoes off the packman topped with a second-hand straw boater, her long brown hair hanging down her back. Now, taller, plumped out, with shiny, short, marcel-waved hair, dressed in a smart brown suit, a cream silk blouse, with dainty brown shoes and pink silk stockings – no wonder Father looked beside himself with pride as he brought her in through the door. Short-sighted Mam blinked her tears away behind her glasses. The warm, scented hug my sister gave me made me feel I was polluting her.

'Quick, goo upstairs and fetch the best spoons and knives down,' Mam whispered urgently to me. Mam kept our best bits of cutlery well polished with brick dust in a cardboard shoe-box on the wash-stand table. There was a mirror over it. The reflection of my very plain face, straight dull hair, steel-rimmed glasses and old frock was too awful: I burst into tears. The strongest emotion was shame that such a beautiful sister had to own such as me.

We all felt a bit shy at the tea table. After tea, too shy to take her arm, I followed a worshipful distance behind my sister as she walked around the top of the village – marvelling at her magnanimity for talking and laughing with the local young chaps. How I bragged about her to my friends at school the next day! About her beauty, her clothes, and the proper nightdress trimmed with lace that she wore to bed.

My little brother and I hurried home from school. Mam told us our sister had walked to town to buy us some fancy cakes for tea; with our adoration increased, we ran through the woodland path to meet her. Her eyes lit up at the sight of us but she looked as though she had been crying.

We walked each side of her in subdued silence for a bit. I couldn't stand it. 'Wot be the matter?' I asked.

She burst into tears. ''Tis Kezzie Larkin. I seen her in town today. She was dressed in long old rags carrying pegs around in a basket wi' a gypsy 'oman. Poor Kezzie, her's nothing but a gypsy now.'

Our Scott

I don't remember when we got him; he was just there, part of the family, a small black and white mongrel, our Scott.

His appetite was very catholic, but the scraps he wheedled from our poor-man's table gave him a prodigious amount of energy. He was a master scrounger. I can still see the swollen veins on the butcher's face when Scott stole a string of sausages from his basket and ran off for safety in the narrow gap between our garden shed and next door's thorny hedge. Poking sticks, well-aimed stones, curses and threats did not deter him from his stolen feast.

The wails from the short-sighted neighbour still ring in my ears. She had put two slices of fish she had fried for tea to keep warm on her steel fender. She found only a well licked plate and Scott sitting by her open cottage door, contentedly smacking his chops.

He landed me into some scrapes with Mam before she started to shut him up in the back kitchen at meal times.

Before that, he would sneak under the table, pushing his head persistently against the legs of us children, begging us to pass him down scraps from our plates. Even ever-hungry Scott turned his nose up at the little dollops of cabbage I dropped down to him from my Sunday dinner-plate. There they still were, soiling the scrubbed stone flags under my chair when Mam cleared up.

He constantly dropped me in trouble at school, too. It was difficult for Mam to keep our cottage door shut with my toddler siblings about. I rarely progressed more than half-way through the long wooded walk to school before he was there, trotting behind my heels, tail wagging madly, ready for school.

'Goo on wum, you naughty dog!' I would scold him. Down went his tail between his legs, his body made an about-turn but his head turned to me, his eyes two brown pools of hurt beyond betrayal.

I couldn't bear it. 'No, no, you be a good dog. I do love ya,' and back he would rush at me, all reproach gone.

Keeping this up all the way to the schoolyard gate was a dreadful hindrance and gave me no option but to leave him looking the picture of misery outside, made worse by his put-on bout of the shivers.

Assembly and scripture lesson would be over and sums begun before I poked my head round the classroom door. A terrible duffer at arithmetic, I copped it from my long-suffering teacher.

'Ah! Miss Sloth has arrived at last! Now we must all wait until she gets to her desk; no need for her to arrive at lessons early, because she never gets a sum right. Oh well, she can have a black mark in her book, and stay in during playtime for an extra arithmetic lesson.'

No good telling teacher about Scott. My burdens were heavy, but his suffering, left scolded and abandoned outside, was much worse.

Though he wasn't allowed to attend school, we considered our Scott a genius. How else could he be clever enough to know when the dog-licence man was coming round the village? When this happened, on his own initiative, Scott hid in the coal-hole in the back kitchen with never a sniff or a whine to betray his presence, so that Mam could look the man straight in the eye and deny we kept a dog. The licence was seven-and-six per annum; we just didn't have that sort of money, and Scott knew it.

Our small living-room and back-kitchen-cum-coal-house were always overcrowded with a crawling baby, toddlers' feet, old Great-Auntie's corn-calloused rheumaticky ones, Mam's busy feet, Dad's heavy boots and the fidgety feet of us bigger ones. But if Scott couldn't find a lap to sit on, he was adept at finding a corner to curl up in out of everybody's way. Ever ready to defend us all, he would growl only when a strange footstep — bar the dog licence man's — approached the door.

Nearly every child's father in our area was a miner, and it was the hungry twenties. Unsurprisingly, when the men went on strike rather than submit to even more inhuman conditions, food scraps became too precious even for well loved dogs.

Father explained to us why he had found another home for Scott. It was with a kindly old pit-butty of his, whose children had grown up and left home for work, and were now able to help their parents out.

Father walked over three miles to take Scott to his new home, where he was given a bellyful of food as the initial bribe to stay. He had returned, almost to our garden gate, when the dog came panting up behind him, and the tear smudges were still on our faces as we welcomed him back.

Father had to be firm. The next day he walked Scott back to his new home. 'Kip'n shut up fr a couple o' days to settle 'un in,' he advised his old friend.

Three days later Scott bounded joyously back through our door.

Father sighed. 'All right then, old bwoy, if thee'st rather starve wi' us lot than live wi' a vull belly zomewhere else, thee shal'st stop 'ere.'

Scott was getting on a bit, but still very agile, when I left home at fourteen to go into domestic service. The strike was over, but not for father.

Pit owners and management had black-listed him for his courage in speaking up against their demands. Mine was one less mouth for Mam to feed but, dreadfully homesick, I lived for the day when I could go home for the holidays.

Not knowing what chores my mistress might want done before I started out, I could not let my family know what time to meet me. When I had walked from the railway halt to the edge of the forest where the woodland path led to our village, I would call, 'Scott, Scott, come on, Scott.'

In a matter of minutes, a small black and white bindle would come bouncing through the ferns, impelled like a small rocket by his own enthusiasm, right into my arms; my herald, to welcome me home. Sensing what his urgent departure meant, my little brothers and sisters would come running in his wake, turning my heart over a little as they pulled up shyly in front of the big sister who had become a bit of a stranger after a year from home.

I was seventeen when I went home for my annual summer holiday from my job in London. At the woodland path I called out for Scott. No Scott came, despite repeated callings. Disappointed, I walked home through the forest.

Disappointment turned into heartache when I stepped indoors; matters had turned from bad to worse. Father still had no job; his loyal butties helped out from their own meagre resources, but sad-eyed and grey-faced, he seemed to have shrunk. So had Mam, and the pot-bellies and skinny legs of the little ones told their own story.

After the hugs and kisses, I sat down to a good meal that, by hook or by crook, Mam had mustered up for my homecoming. 'Where's our Scott?' I asked.

Father took a time to answer. 'I be afeared, my wench, that we an't'n any more. The poor old bwoy was in a bad shape. No doubt 'im could 'a' gone on a bit longer if we could 'a' give 'im the right sort o' victuals, but 'twas cruel to let'n goo on. 'Is poor legs was givin' out, an' 'im was sufferin'.'

Our way of life had not included such luxuries as the service of a vet. I sensed that it had been Dad's job to put Scott out of his misery. I knew that father, intelligent and utterly humane, would have thought of the most merciful way. Just then I could not harass him further to find out.

Mam pushed my plate of food towards me, but it was not easy to swallow with no warm head pushing my knees under the table.